A Mark Dahle Portfolio

Monkey Brains On Big Mountain

Little Gibbon's Big Adventures #3

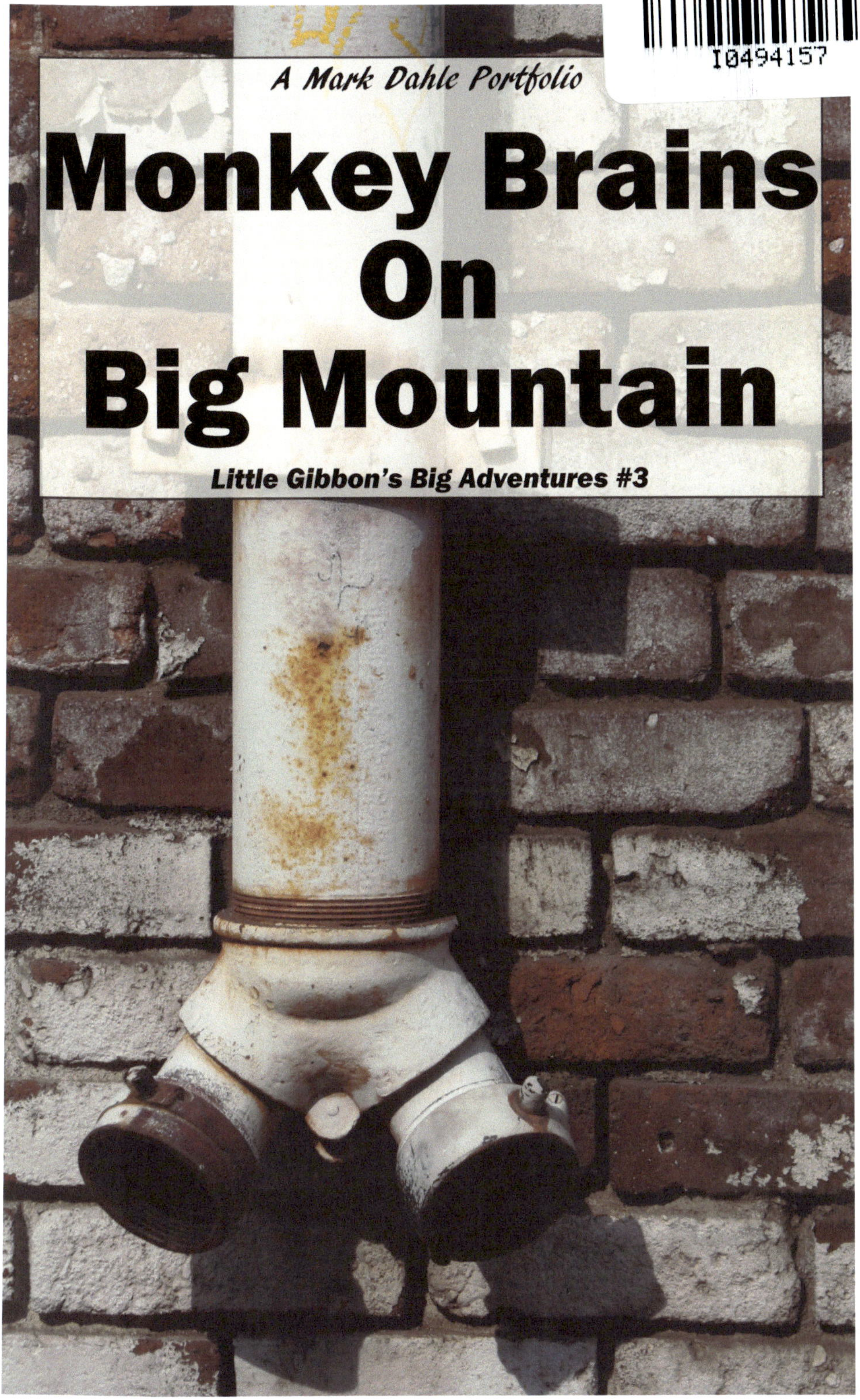

This is the third story about a gibbon who liked adventures. All the other gibbons called him Monkey Brains.

Books in this series include:
1. Monkey Brains On Big River
2. Monkey Brains On Big Ocean
3. Monkey Brains On Big Mountain
4. Monkey Brains In Big Desert

~ ~ ~

Mark Dahle Portfolios can be read in a few minutes and enjoyed for a lifetime.

Unlike many picture books, the text in this book is not related to the art. This might seem weird at first. One thing that makes it better is to order more portfolios until you get used to it. Fortunately, space is provided on the pages for you to draw your own pictures of Big Mountain if you like.

This portfolio includes a beautiful 36 x 24 inch painting (at the right), twenty-four great photos from Spokane, Washington, and a story about an adventurer who called himself Little Gibbon.

Photographs in this book are available in limited editions. See http://www.MarkDahle.com for more information and for previews of upcoming portfolios.

We do our best to create portfolios free of editing mistakes. But it's hard to catch everything. We reward people who report errors in any Mark Dahle portfolio. For details see MarkDahle.com/Typos.html or email MarkDahle@aol.com with the subject line "Typos." Thanks!

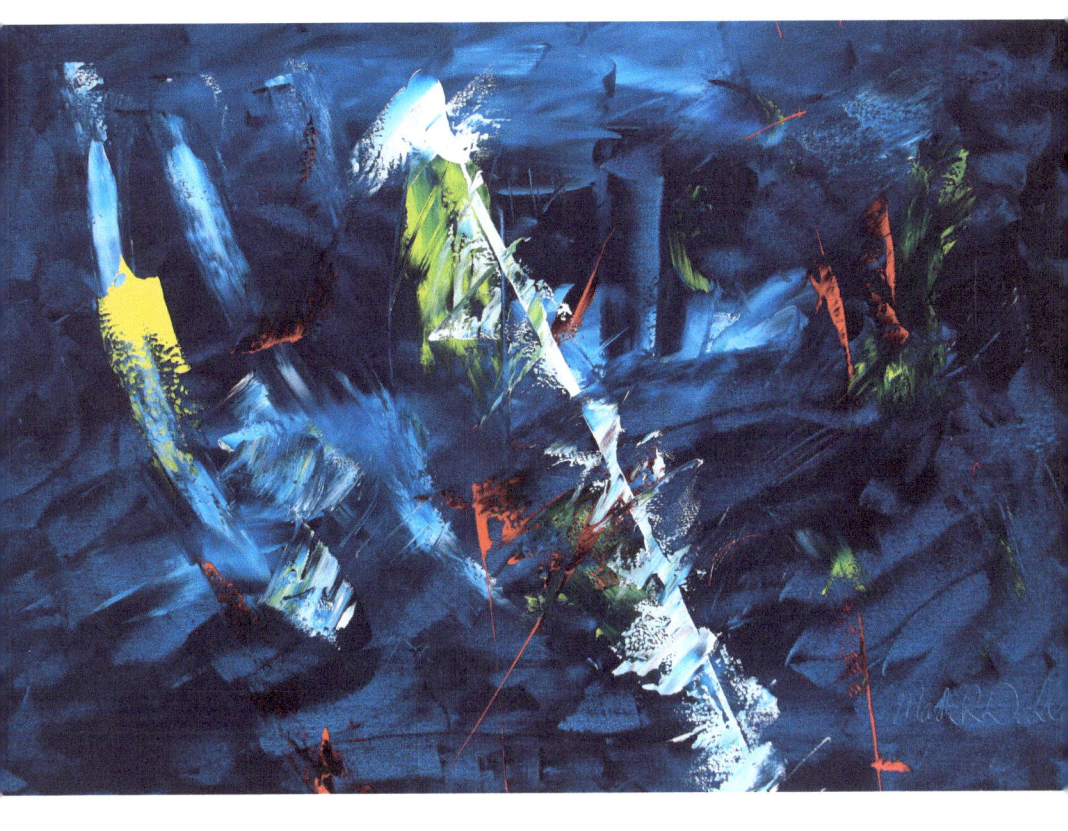

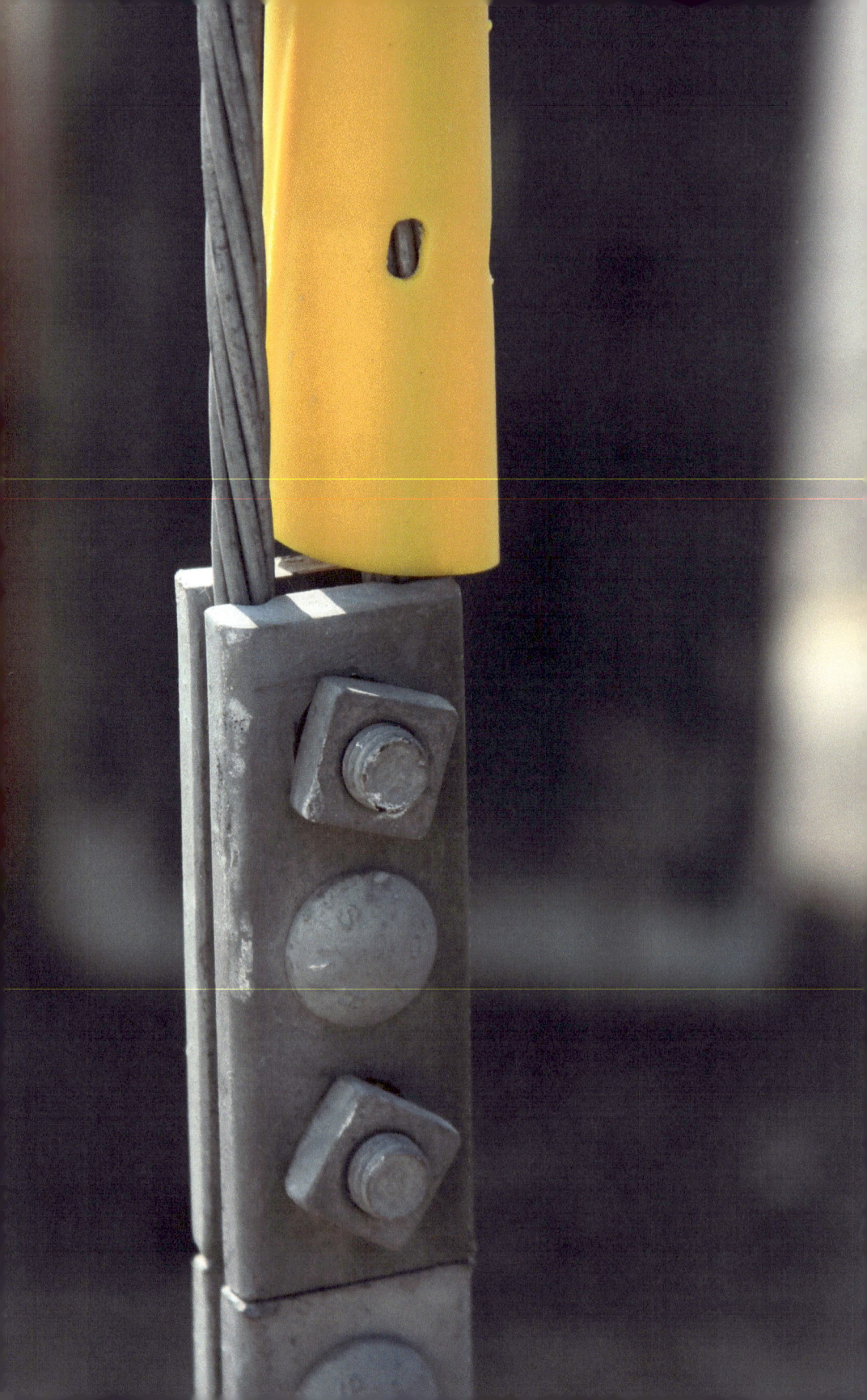

Gibbons usually like to swing from tree to tree. But the youngest gibbon in one family preferred adventures instead. He would swing in trees if it would get him to a new adventure. Otherwise he wasn't interested. As a result, all the gibbons he knew called him Monkey Brains. He called himself Little Gibbon, since he was still growing and learning lots.

One morning he woke up in his canoe, surprised to find he was on dry land, several feet above the low tide mark. He hopped out and pulled his canoe farther ashore.

The day before, Little Gibbon had been on Big Ocean. Today he wanted another adventure, but he needed a paddle before he went back on Big Ocean, and his paddle was on a bank of Big River, many miles away.

If Little Gibbon wasn't going on Big Ocean today, where could he go instead? He looked inland. Big Mountain was close by.

"Big Mountain," Little Gibbon cried happily. "We're going to have an adventure!"

Big Mountain smiled. She liked Little Gibbon. When he was around, she could never tell what would happen next.

Before long, Little Gibbon was hiking on a trail at the base of Big Mountain. Little Gibbon didn't have a map. He didn't have any water. He didn't have any food.

It was just like he hadn't learned anything at all!

Little Gibbon didn't care. Who needs a map, water and food when you want to have an adventure, he thought.

Maybe you know the answer already.

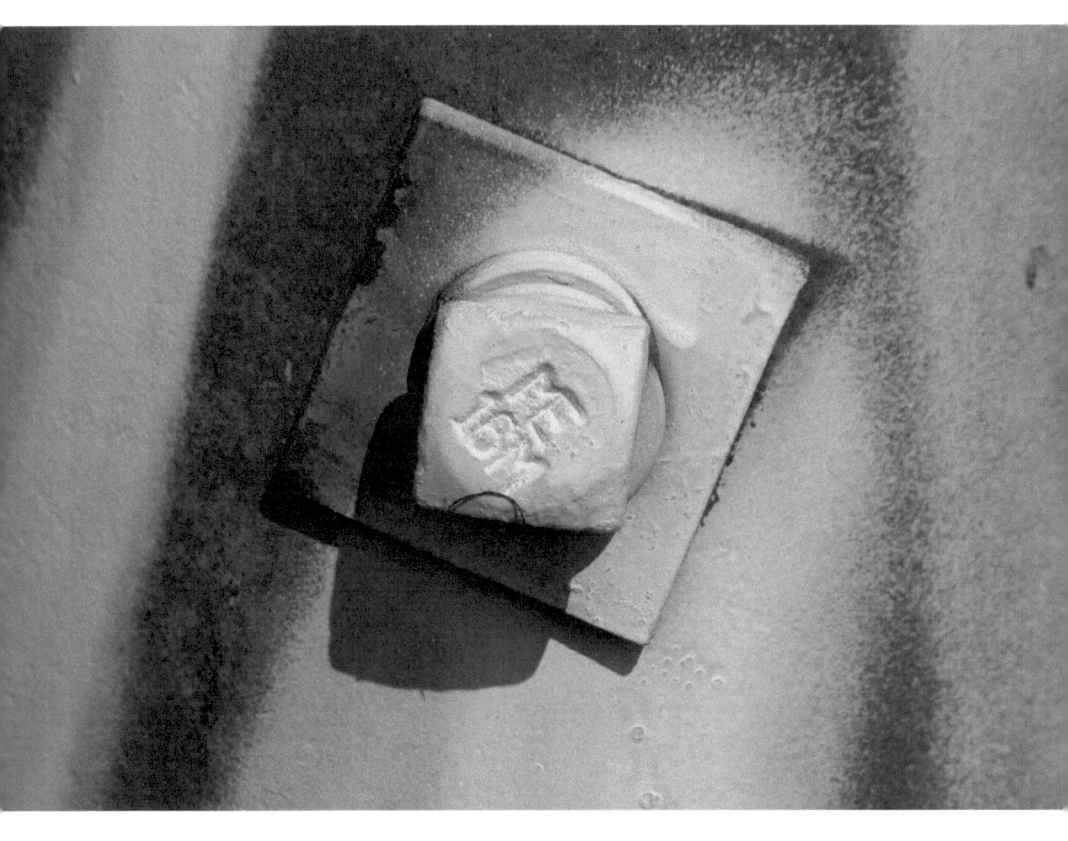

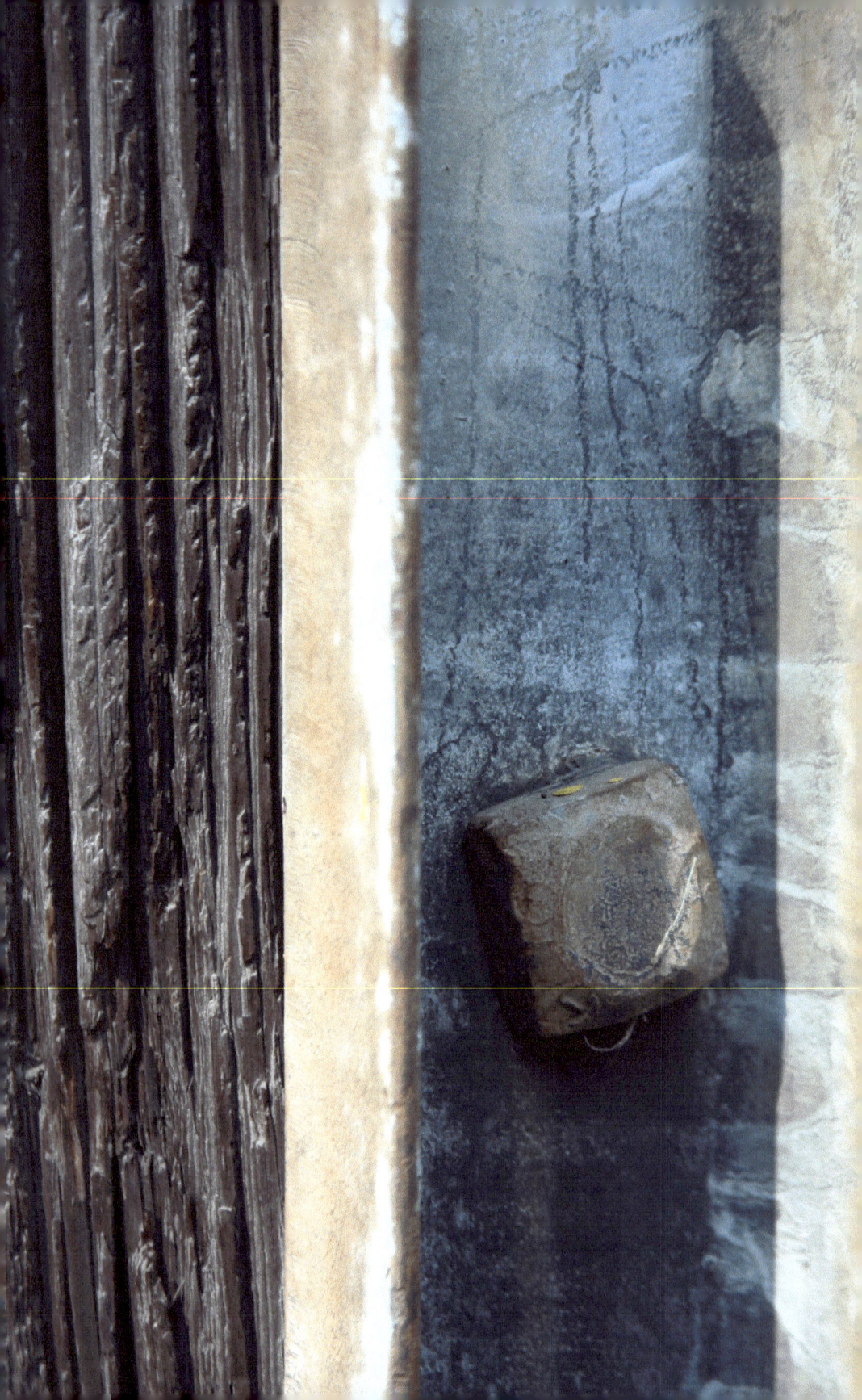

The sun was shining, the air was cool and Big Mountain looked beautiful. On Big Mountain the weather could change in less than an hour, but at the moment things couldn't be nicer. There was very little danger, unless Little Gibbon got lost.

The path Little Gibbon was on headed straight to the Confusing Intersection Of Many Trails.

"Big Mountain," Little Gibbon shouted. "We're having an adventure!"

Before he knew it, Little Gibbon found himself at an intersection. Five new trails spread out before him. Little Gibbon didn't have a map. Which should he choose?

Little Gibbon didn't care. He was having an adventure! Any of them would do! He picked the steepest and started scrambling up Big Mountain.

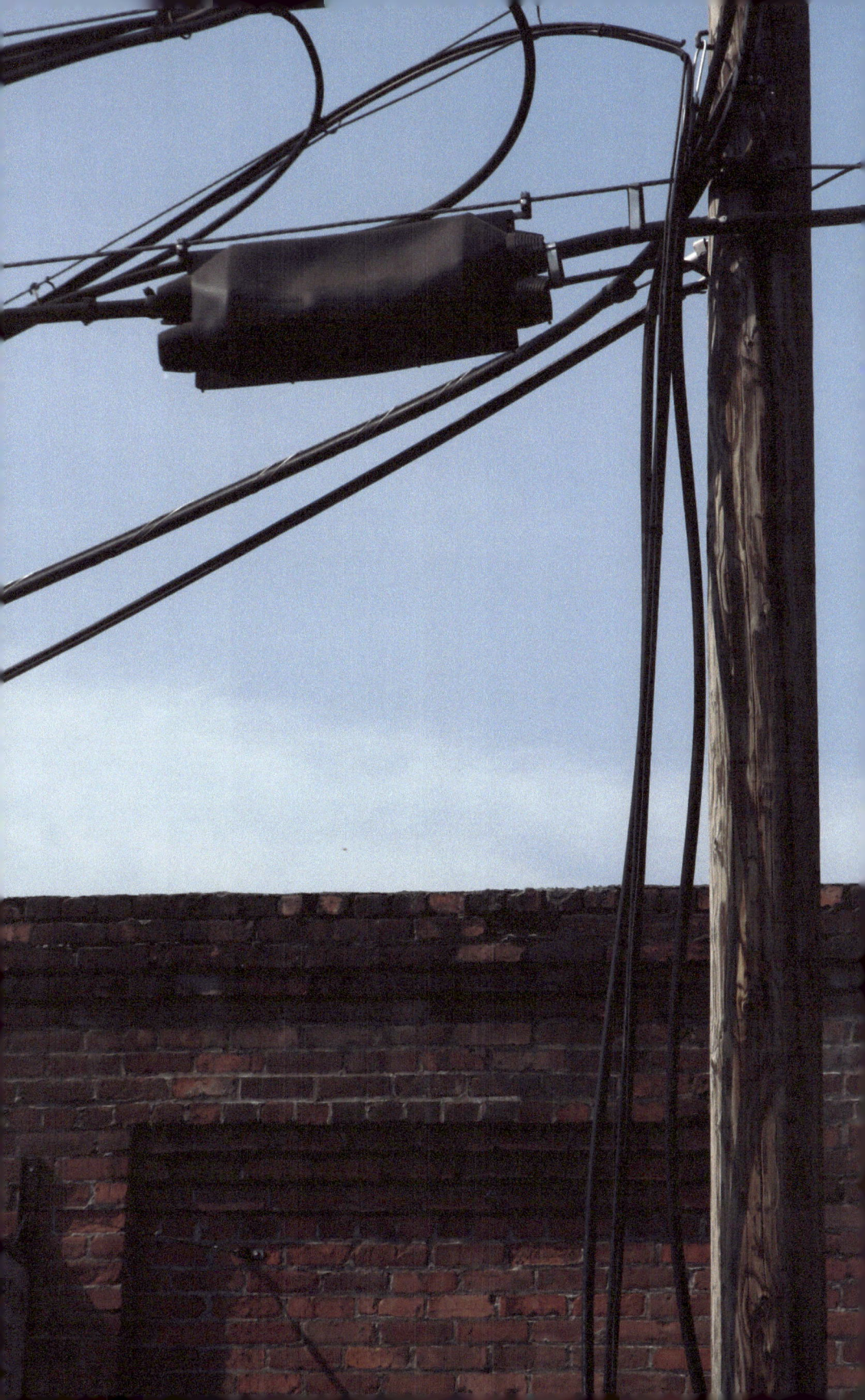

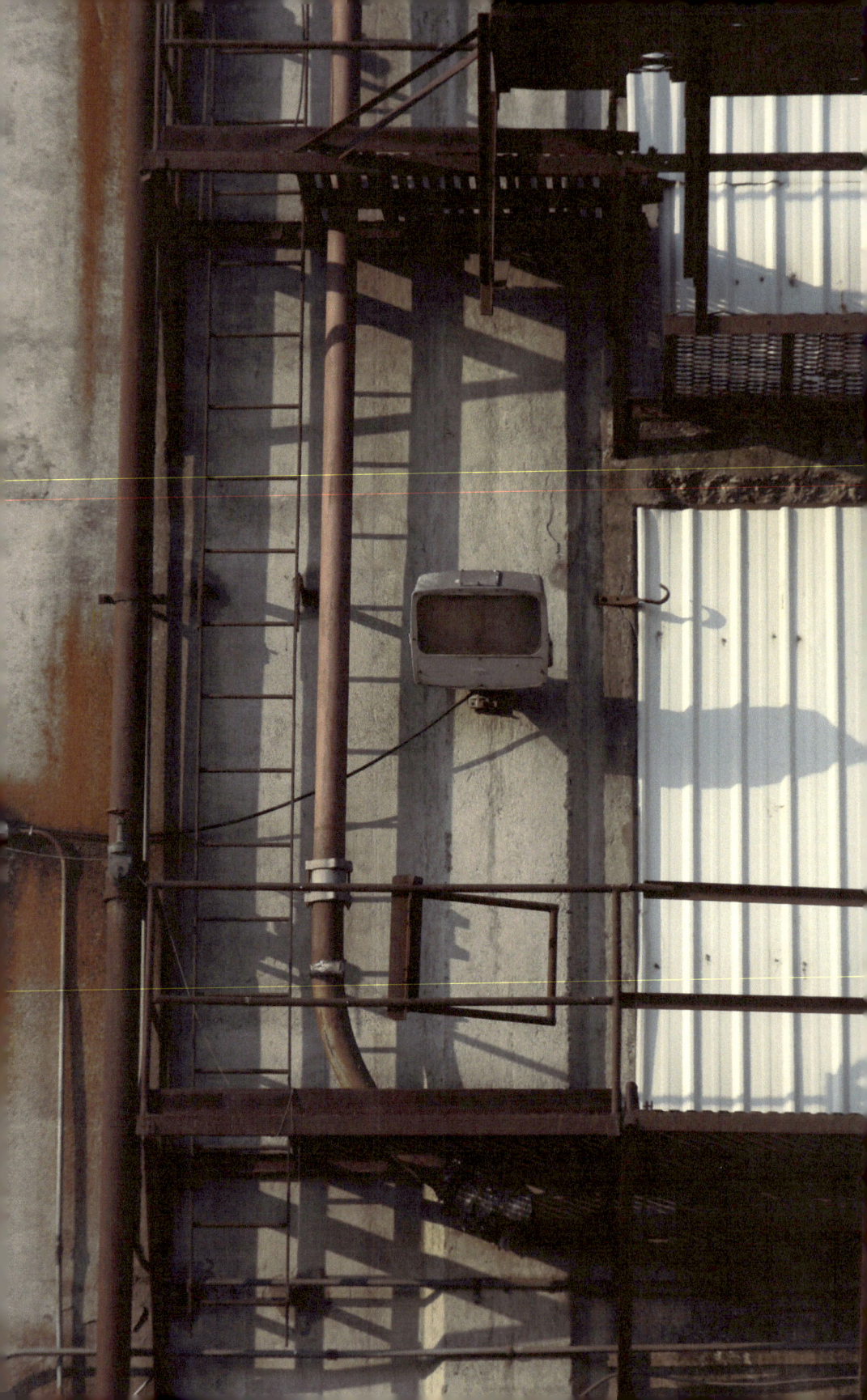

Soon Little Gibbon came to another intersection, this time of three trails. He picked one and quickly came to *another* intersection, this one of seven trails. And soon after that he came to an intersection of two trails. Before he knew it, Little Gibbon couldn't remember which combination of trails would get him back to his canoe. He was lost.

After a moment, Little Gibbon decided he didn't care. He wanted to go *up* Big Mountain, not down. He kept climbing.

Big Mountain smiled. Now that Little Gibbon was safely through the Confusing Intersection Of Many Trails, there was very little danger unless he headed into the Valley Of Angry Bears.

Little Gibbon looked ahead. On his left was a valley filled with fir trees. It looked pleasant. He could hear a distant roaring. Little Gibbon was thirsty and he thought the roaring sounded like a waterfall. "I'd like a drink," Little Gibbon said. "I'll go off the trail and head straight toward the waterfall in that valley."

"Big Mountain!" Little Gibbon cried. Perhaps you want to say it with him. "We're having an adventure!"

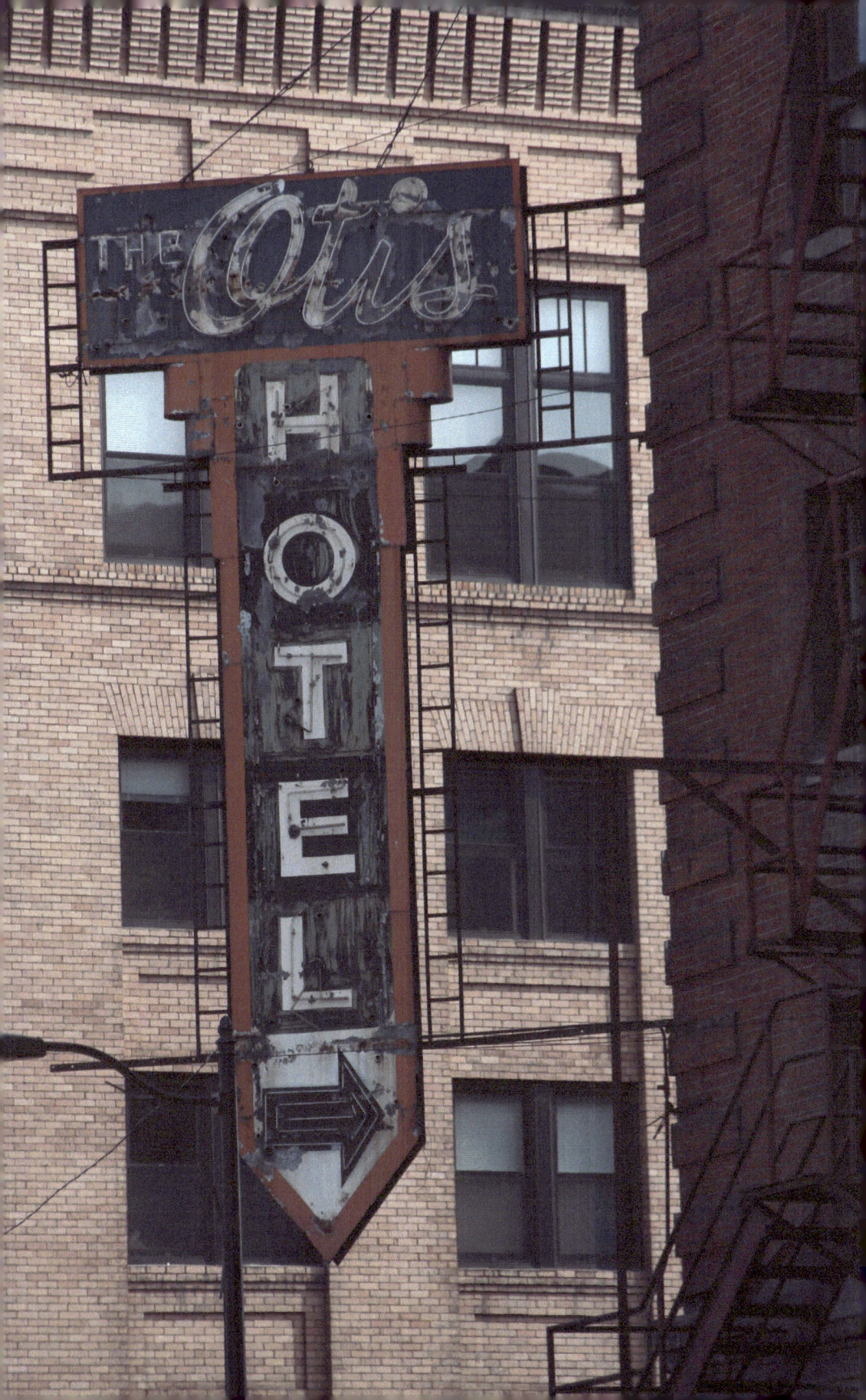

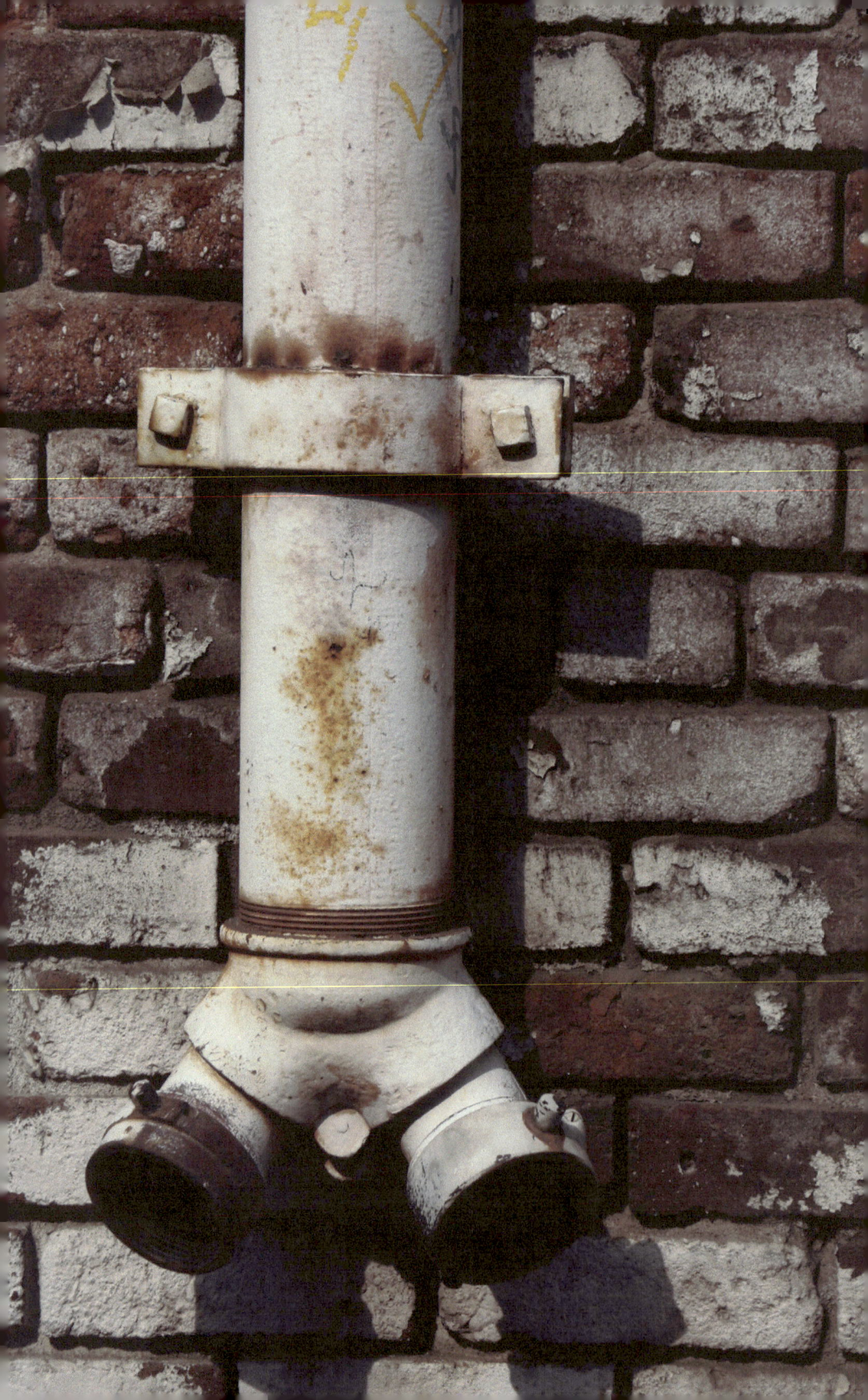

Big Mountain looked down and gasped. Little Gibbon was heading straight toward the biggest group of Angry Bears in the valley.

The roaring was getting louder and louder. Little Gibbon was thinking happily about how thirsty he was and how good it would be to come to a nice waterfall. He was about to step into a clearing when it finally dawned on him that the noise he was hearing didn't sound much like water crashing on rocks. It sounded more like a noise made by a big animal. Or *many* big animals.

Little Gibbon peeked around a tree and looked into the clearing. He was startled to see a huge Angry Bear, roaring. He looked left. He saw two more Angry Bears roaring. He looked right. Three more! And in the distance past them, another five! All of them angry and all of them roaring and all of them looking hungry! Then he saw even more bears farther away! And – he almost jumped – he saw some bears *closer* than he had noticed before. Little Gibbon counted twenty-four very Angry Bears!

Little Gibbon was almost shaking from fear. He tried to be very quiet, but when he backed up he stepped on a twig and it snapped.

Little Gibbon froze. Luckily for him, the bears were roaring so loudly they didn't hear it.

Little Gibbon bolted and ran out of the valley as quickly as he could.

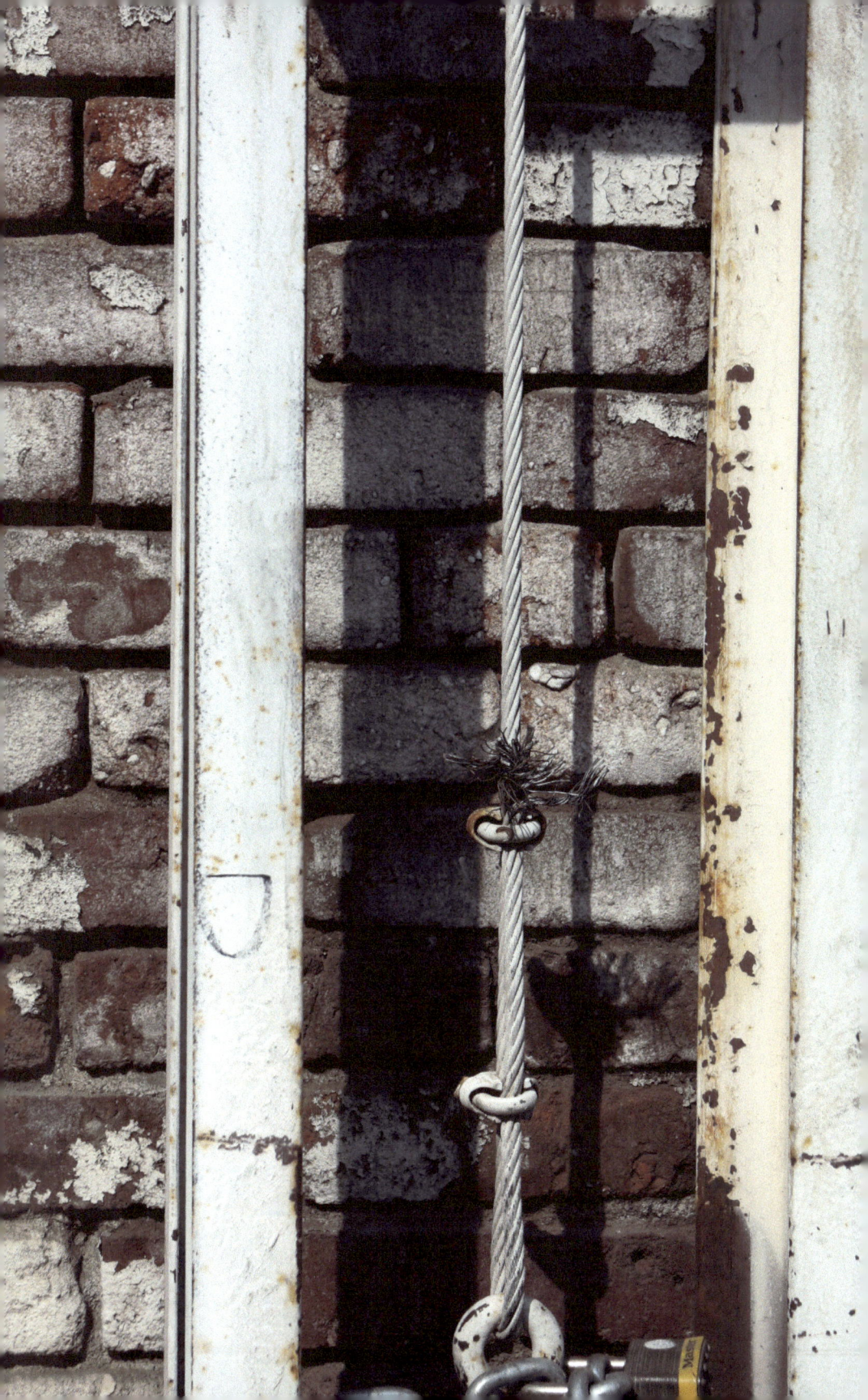

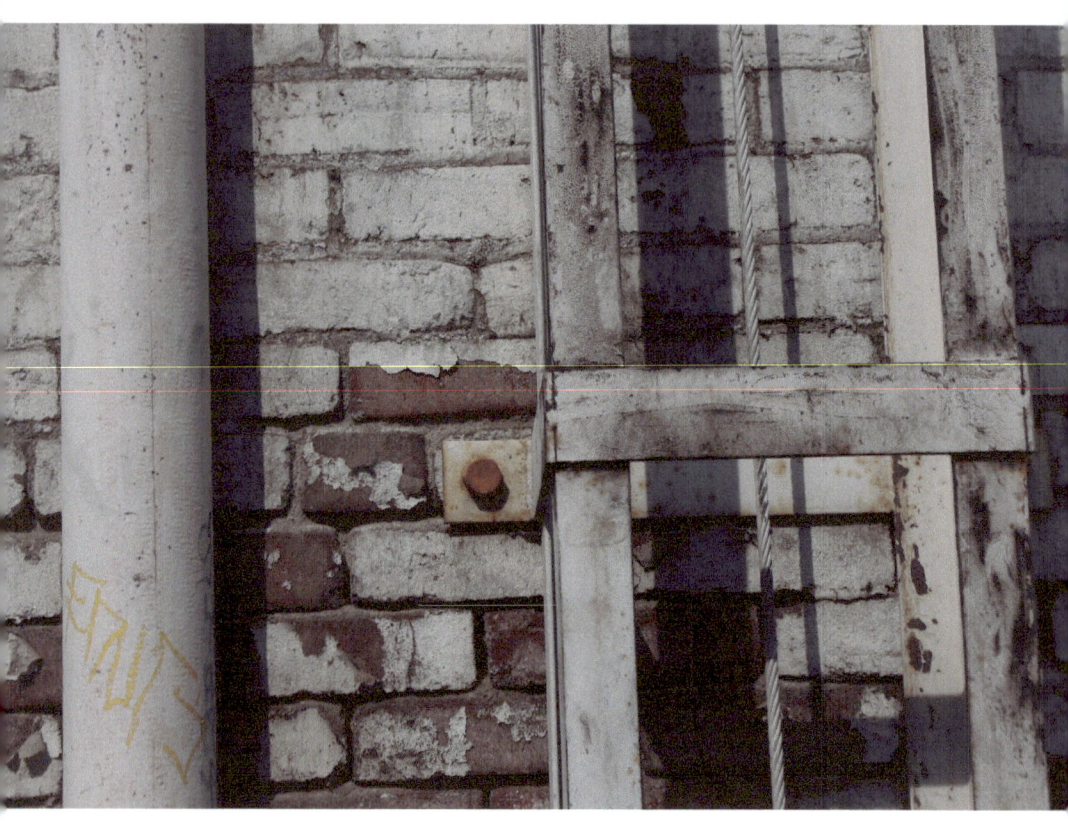

Big Wind had been blowing from the valley toward Little Gibbon, so the bears hadn't smelled him yet. But when Little Gibbon was running away, Big Wind decided to change direction. "I've helped Little Gibbon enough," he said.

Luckily, by the time the bears noticed the scent of Little Gibbon, he was long gone.

Big Mountain smiled. Now that Little Gibbon was safely through the Confusing Intersection Of Many Trails and was out of the Valley Of Angry Bears, there was very little danger unless he climbed Avalanche Cliff.

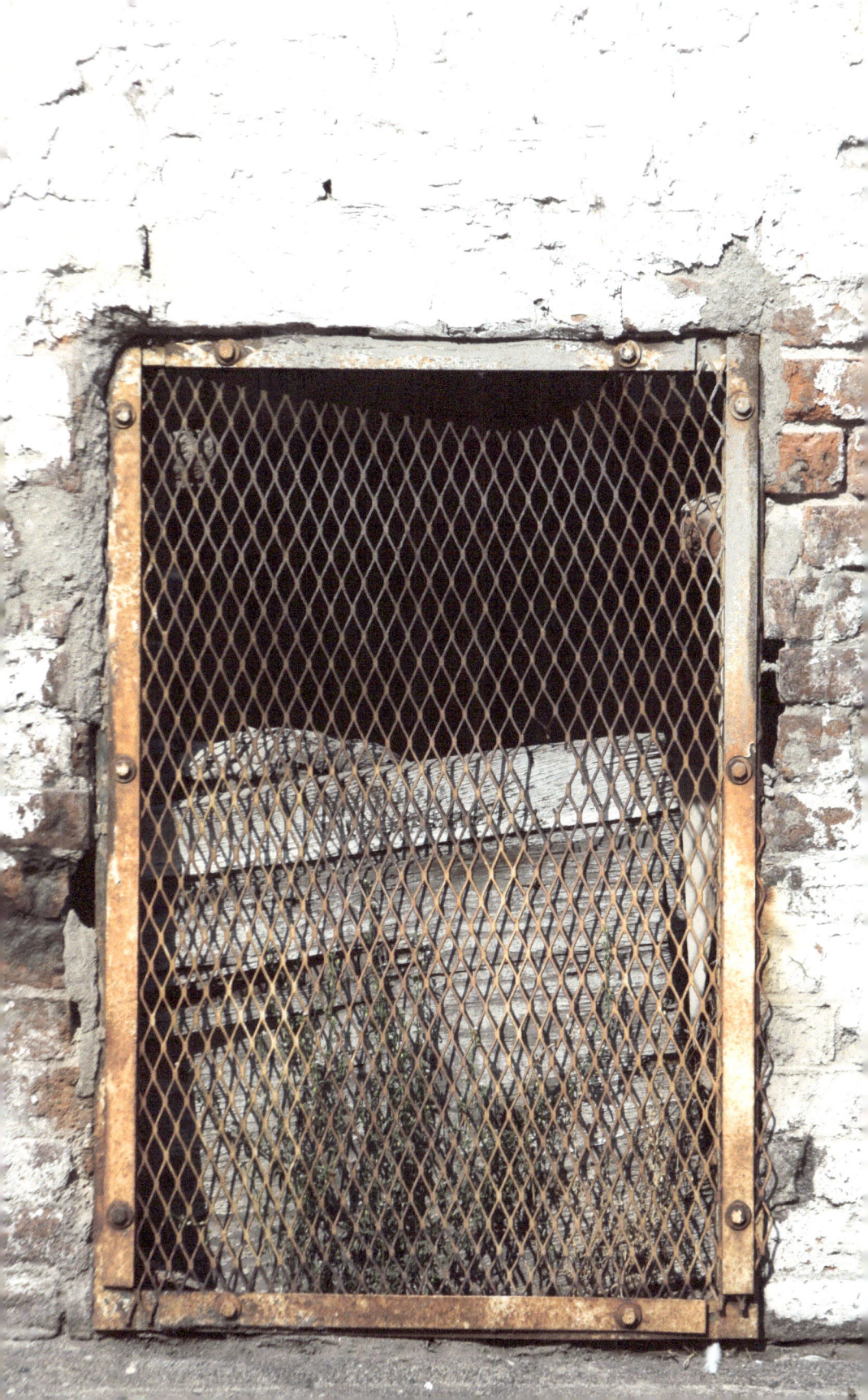

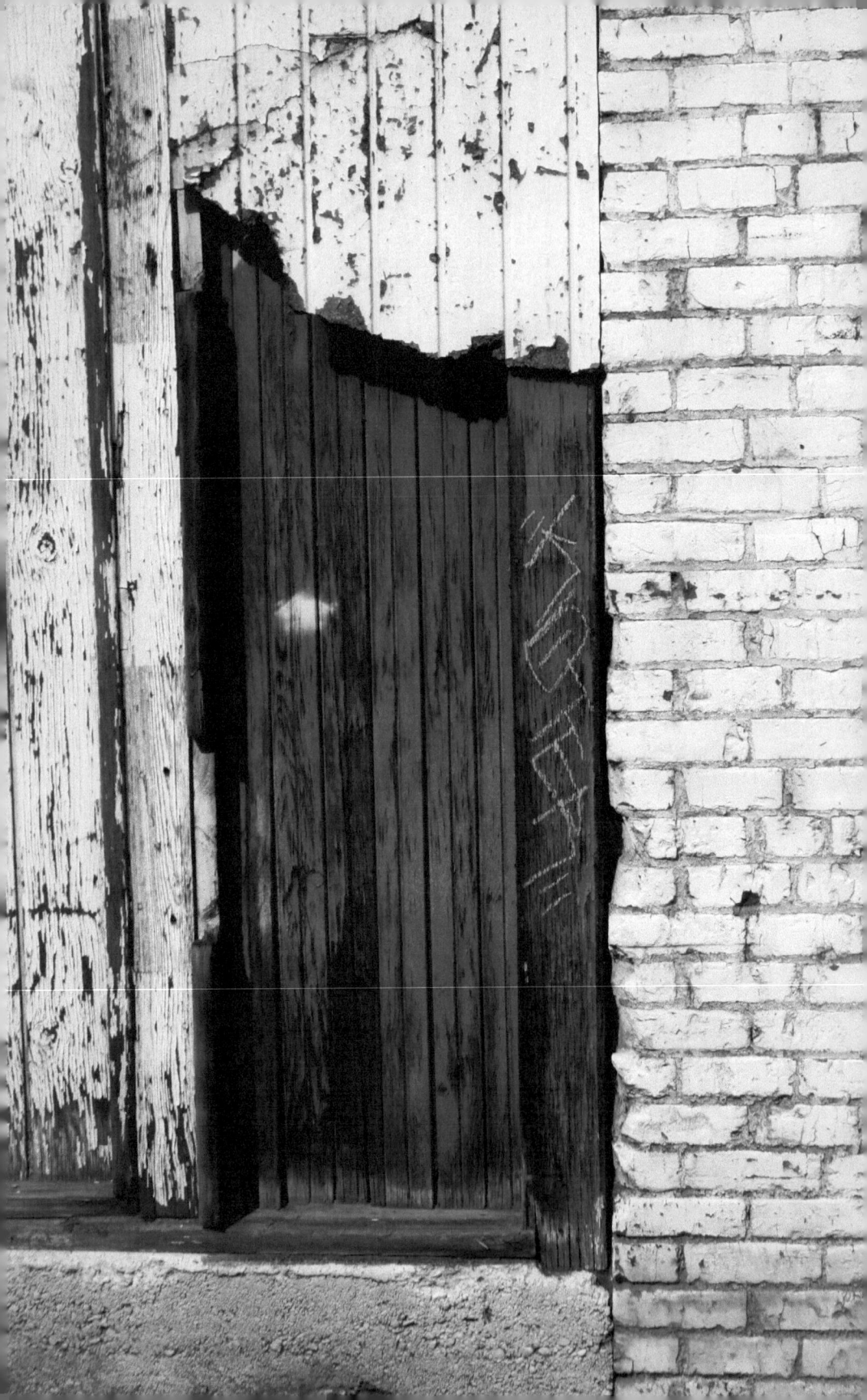

Little Gibbon looked at all the trails he could take next. One went straight through the Valley and passed the Angry Bears. He didn't want *that* trail! Another went back down Big Mountain. He didn't want *that* trail. He also rejected a trail heading to the left and a trail heading to the right. He looked eagerly straight up. He could see a cliff with no trail. If he scrambled straight up the cliff, he could get up Big Mountain faster.

Little Gibbon headed for the cliff.

"Big Mountain," Little Gibbon cried, "We're having an adventure!"

Normally Big Mountain liked to hear Little Gibbon yell things like this. But this time, Little Gibbon was nearly in the middle of Avalanche Cliff. Big Mountain hoped the noise wouldn't start a rockslide.

Meanwhile, Little Gibbon was having so much fun he decided to throw a rock down the hill. But before Little Gibbon could throw his rock, a raven flew by cawing a warning.

The raven flew so close to Little Gibbon that Little Gibbon almost slipped. When he caught his balance, he dislodged a tiny pebble. It bounced down the hill. It was soon joined by a few more pebbles. Then a few more. Then a lot more.

Little Gibbon's eyes got wide. The cliff he was on was an avalanche area! He put the rock he was going to throw very gently back on the steep hillside. He quit trying to climb up. He slowly and gingerly started moving across the face of the cliff, trying to get to the trees on one side. He didn't breathe easily until he was back in the treeline.

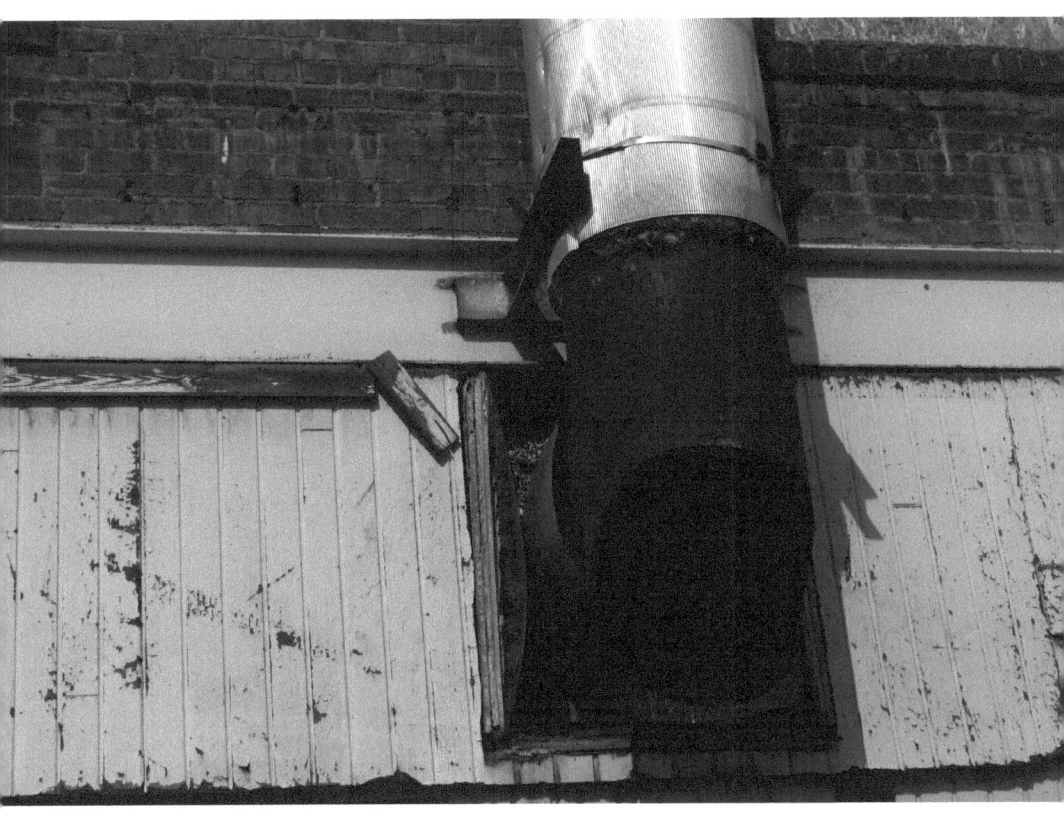

Big Mountain sighed with relief. Now that Little Gibbon was safely through the Confusing Intersection Of Many Trails and had avoided the Valley Of Angry Bears and was no longer on Avalanche Cliff, there was very little danger as long as he didn't go through Hypothermia Pass.

"Big Mountain!" Little Gibbon cried. "We're having an adventure!"

Little Gibbon looked around to see where he would go next. He wanted to find out what was on the back side of the mountain. And the easiest way there was straight ahead, through a pass.

Big Mountain sighed. If Little Gibbon had a map he would have known he was headed straight for Hypothermia Pass.

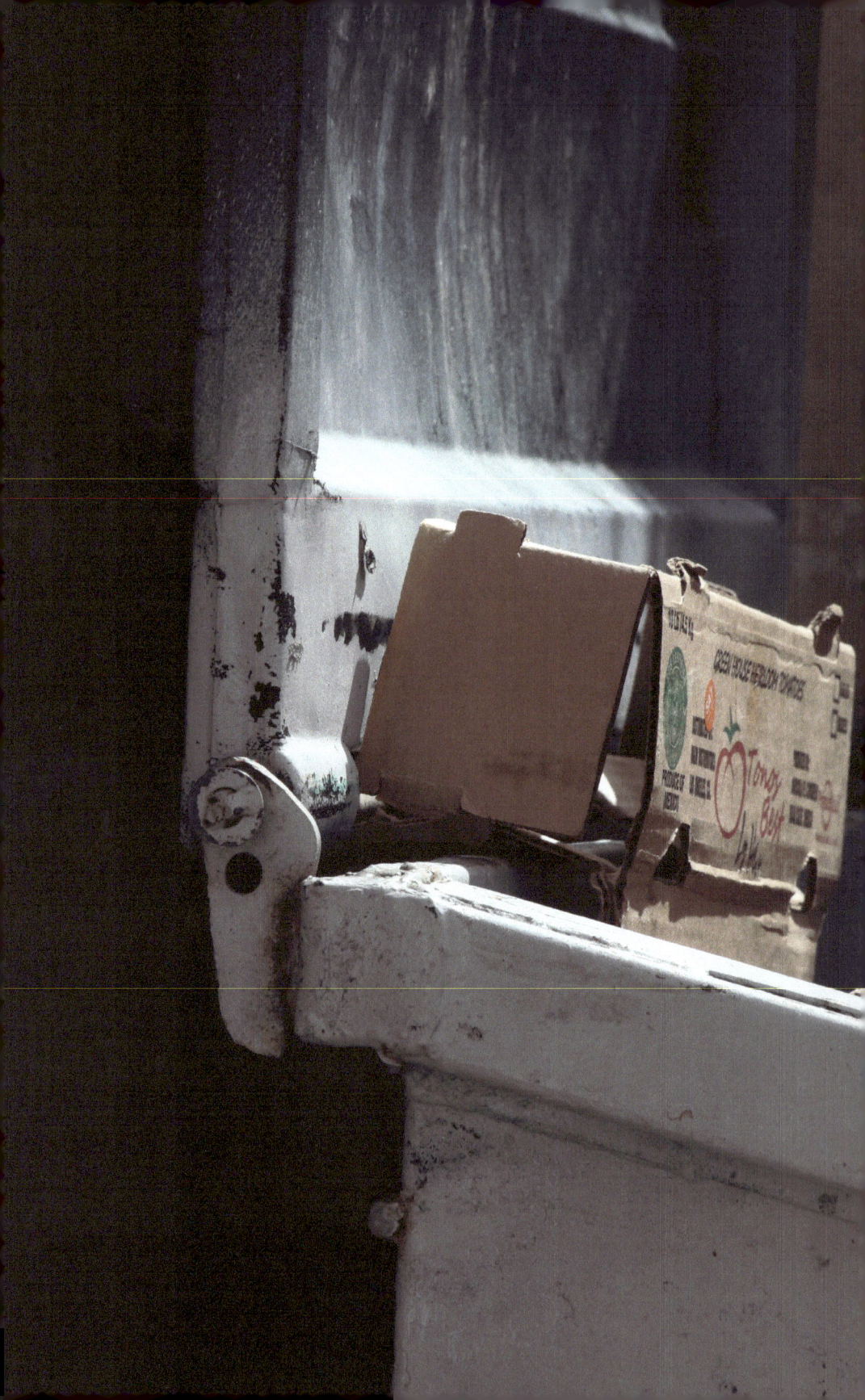

The closer Little Gibbon got to the pass, the stronger and colder Big Wind got.

"Big Wind!" Little Gibbon shouted. "You helped me a lot today and yesterday. Thank you! But I don't think you're helping me that much right now."

Big Wind ignored him. Big Wind was in no mood to be bothered if Little Gibbon was foolish enough to travel through Hypothermia Pass. This was Big Wind's favorite place to play.

Big Wind was raging and blustering and thinking of releasing a pelting rain. He was not going to calm down. At least not today. He was thinking he had been polite for too long.

Little Gibbon was shivering. "I wish I hadn't lost my jacket on Big River," he said. "Big Mountain, this is almost *too much* of an adventure!"

Little Gibbon was cold, cold, cold. That was *before* the Pelting Rains started. Big Mountain hoped Little Gibbon could make it safely through the pass.

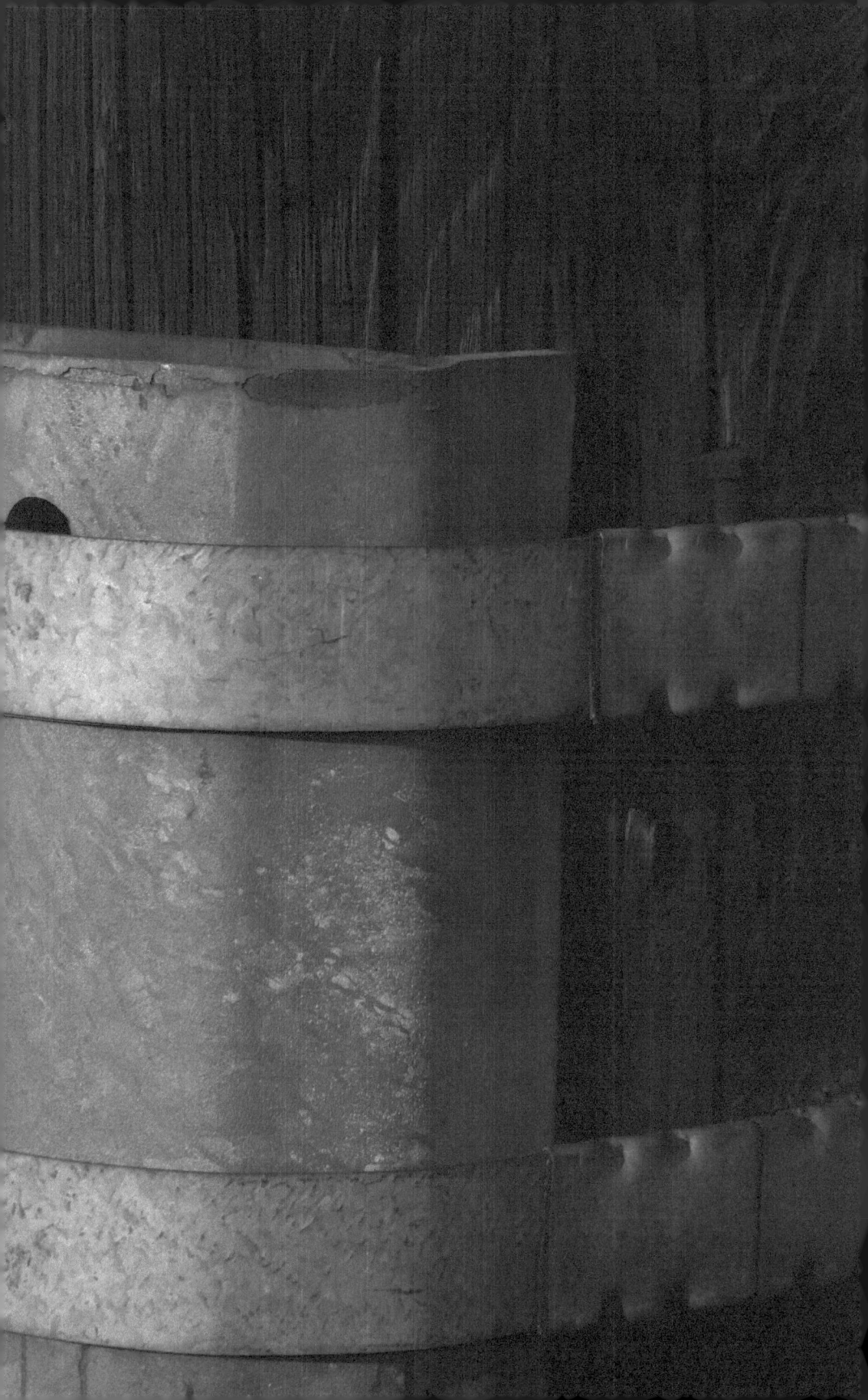

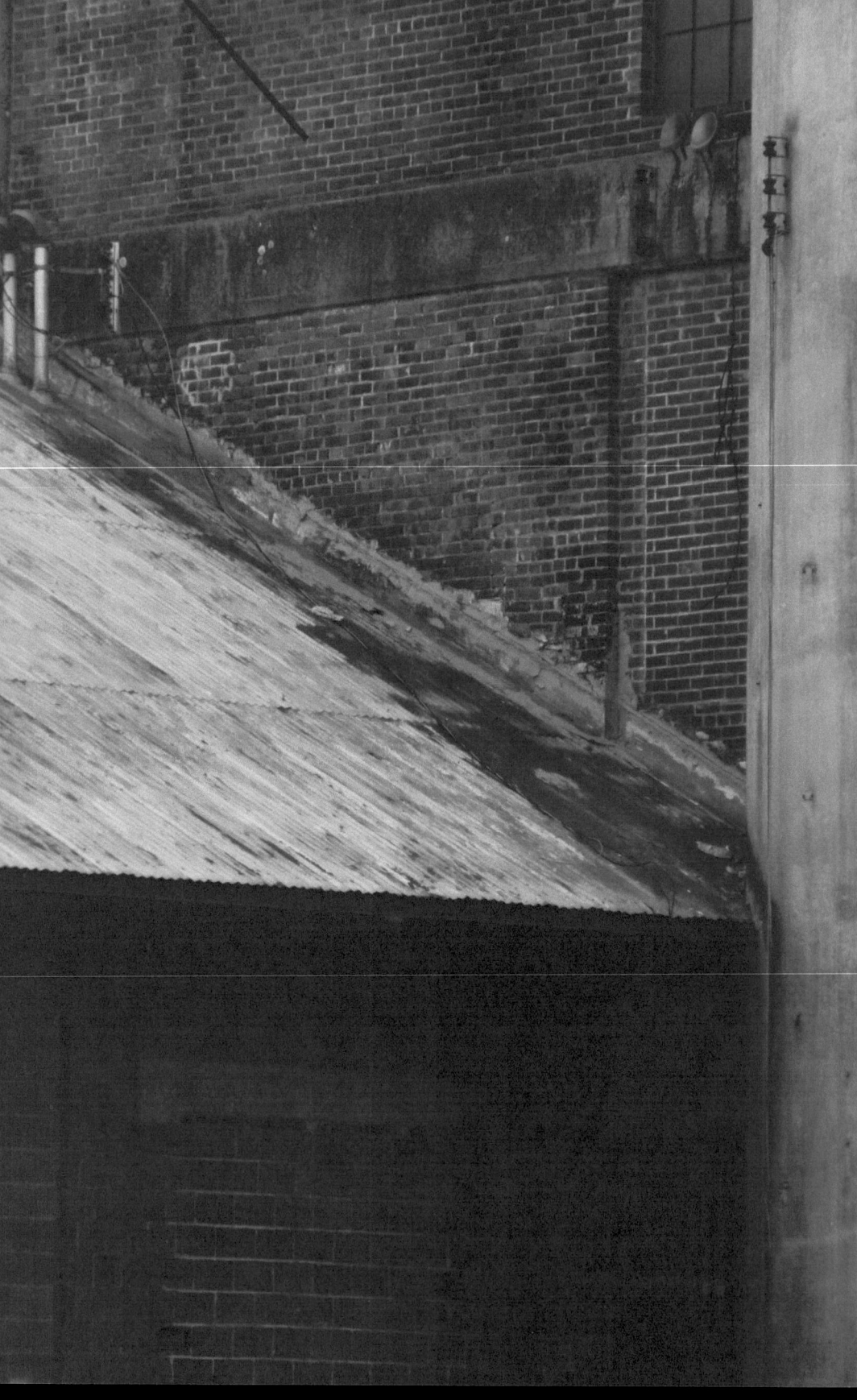

Little Gibbon didn't have food, water, a map or a raincoat. His teeth were chattering, and he was freezing. But he was *not* going to stop in Hypothermia Pass. It was too wet! And too cold! Little Gibbon walked as fast as he could until he was safe from Big Wind on the back side of Big Mountain.

When Little Gibbon saw a cabin, he hurried straight toward it. The cabin was quite plain, but it had a simple desk, a sagging bed, a fireplace, firewood, some kindling and two matches.

Little Gibbon was shivering so much he broke the first match. But with the second match he was able to light the kindling in the fireplace. Then he put some firewood on the kindling and soon he had a roaring fire.

In a few minutes Little Gibbon wasn't shivering any longer. A few minutes after that, Little Gibbon was quite warm. And a few minutes after that, he was so comfortable he fell asleep on the sagging bed. It was time for his nap.

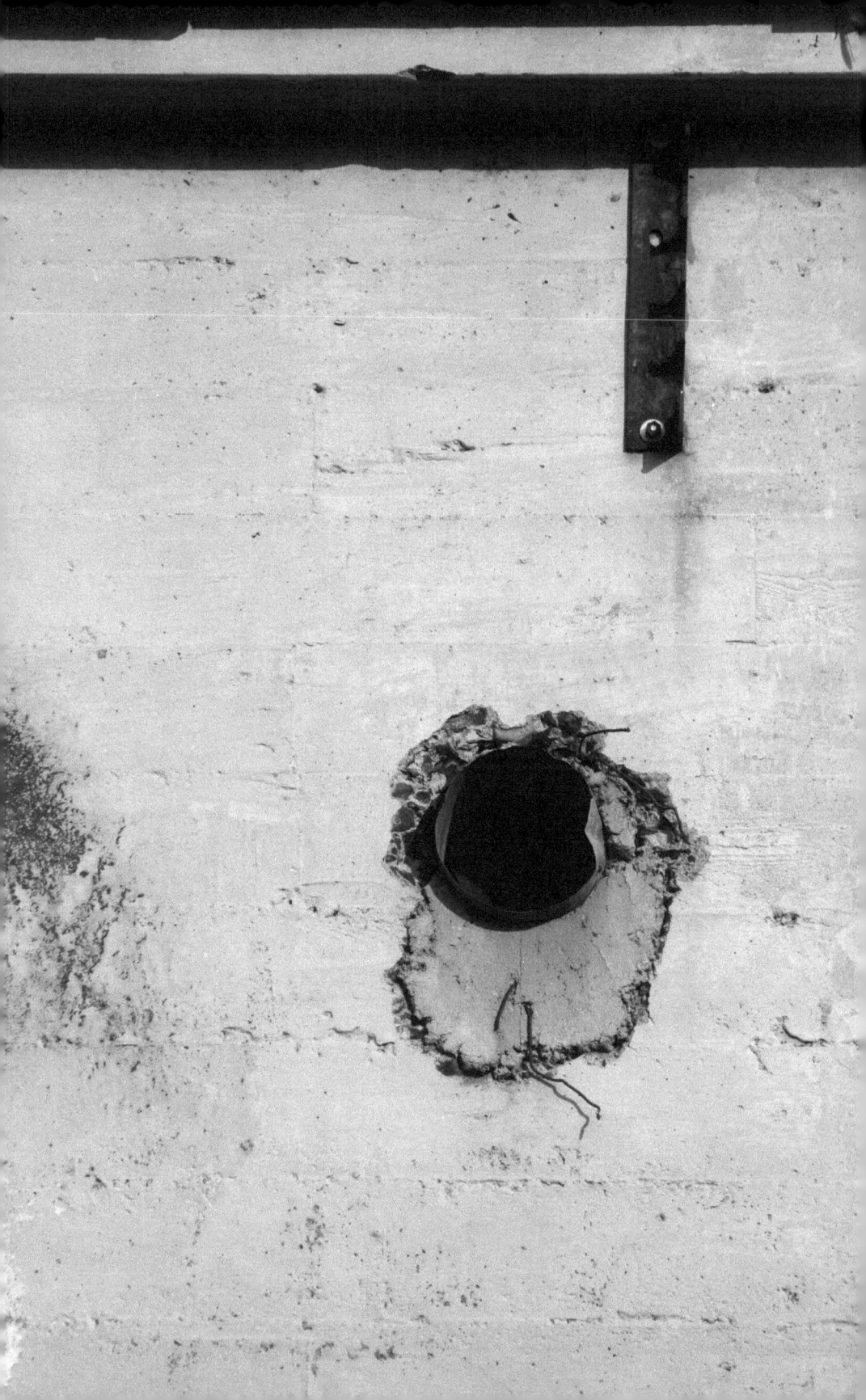

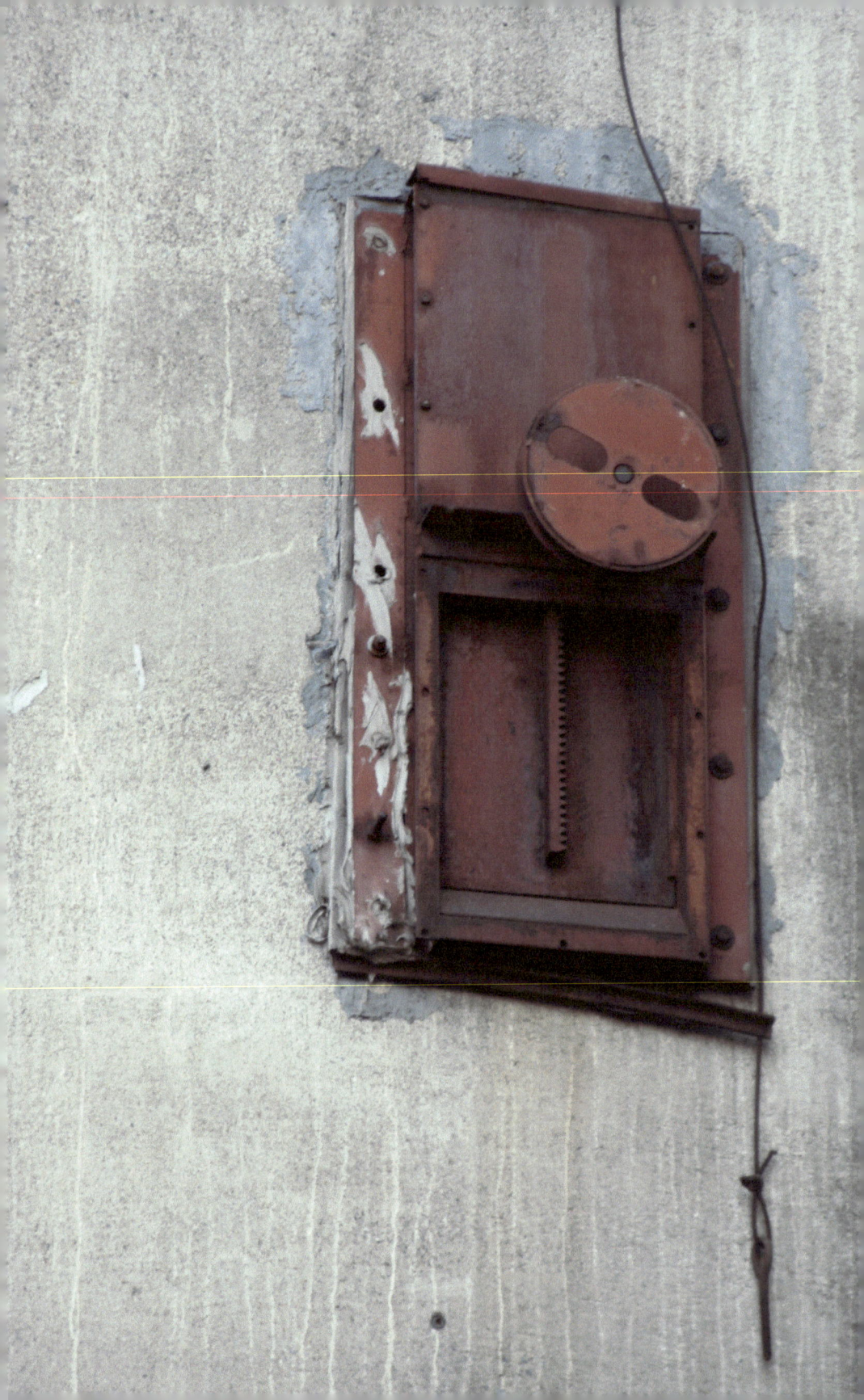

Big Mountain smiled. It looked like Little Gibbon had had enough adventures for one day.

Big Mountain didn't wake Little Gibbon when the Pelting Rains turned to Freezing Sleet and then became a Tree Threatening Ice Storm. Little Gibbon slept while tree branches fell all around the cabin, crashing to the ground because of the weight of the ice.

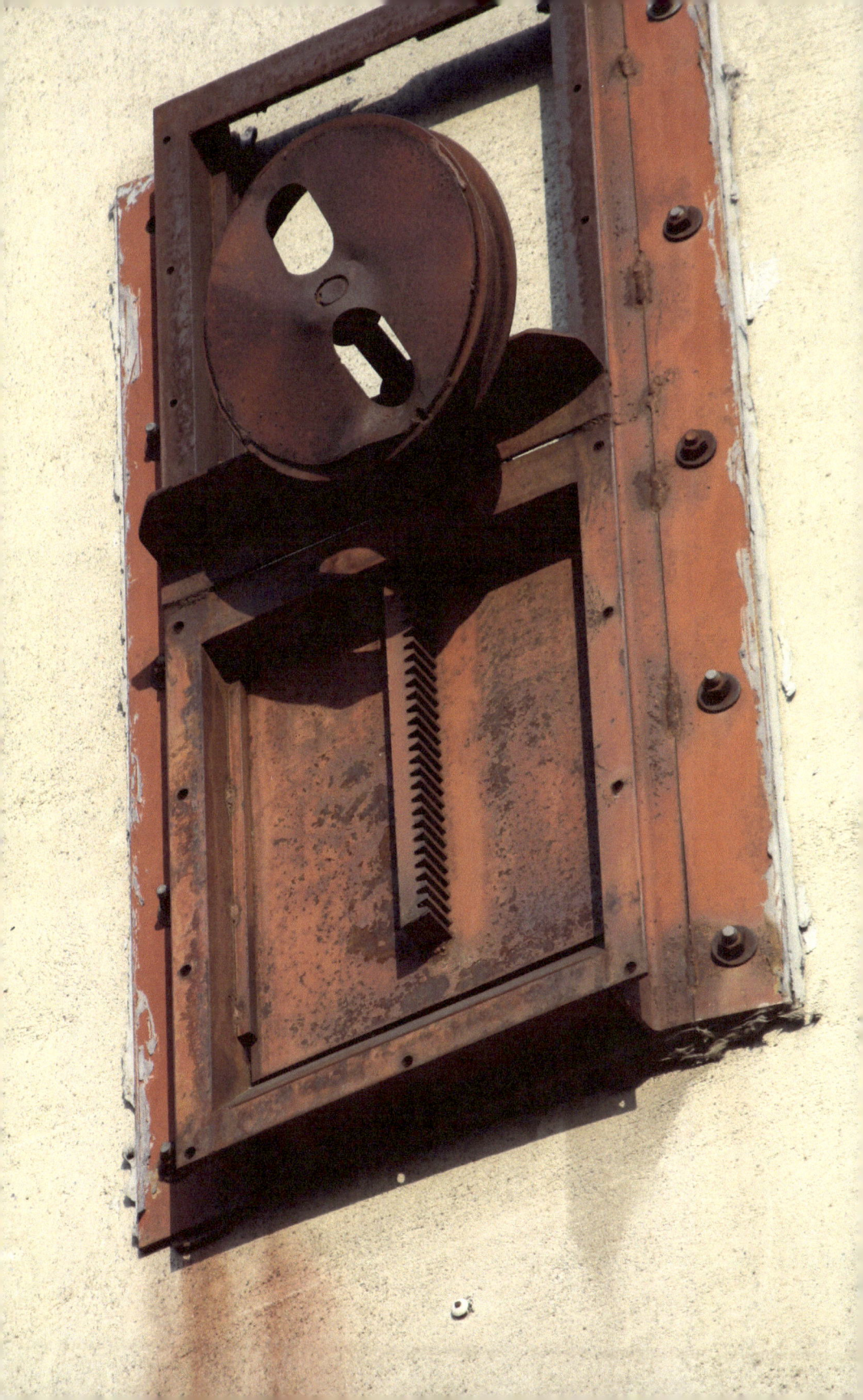

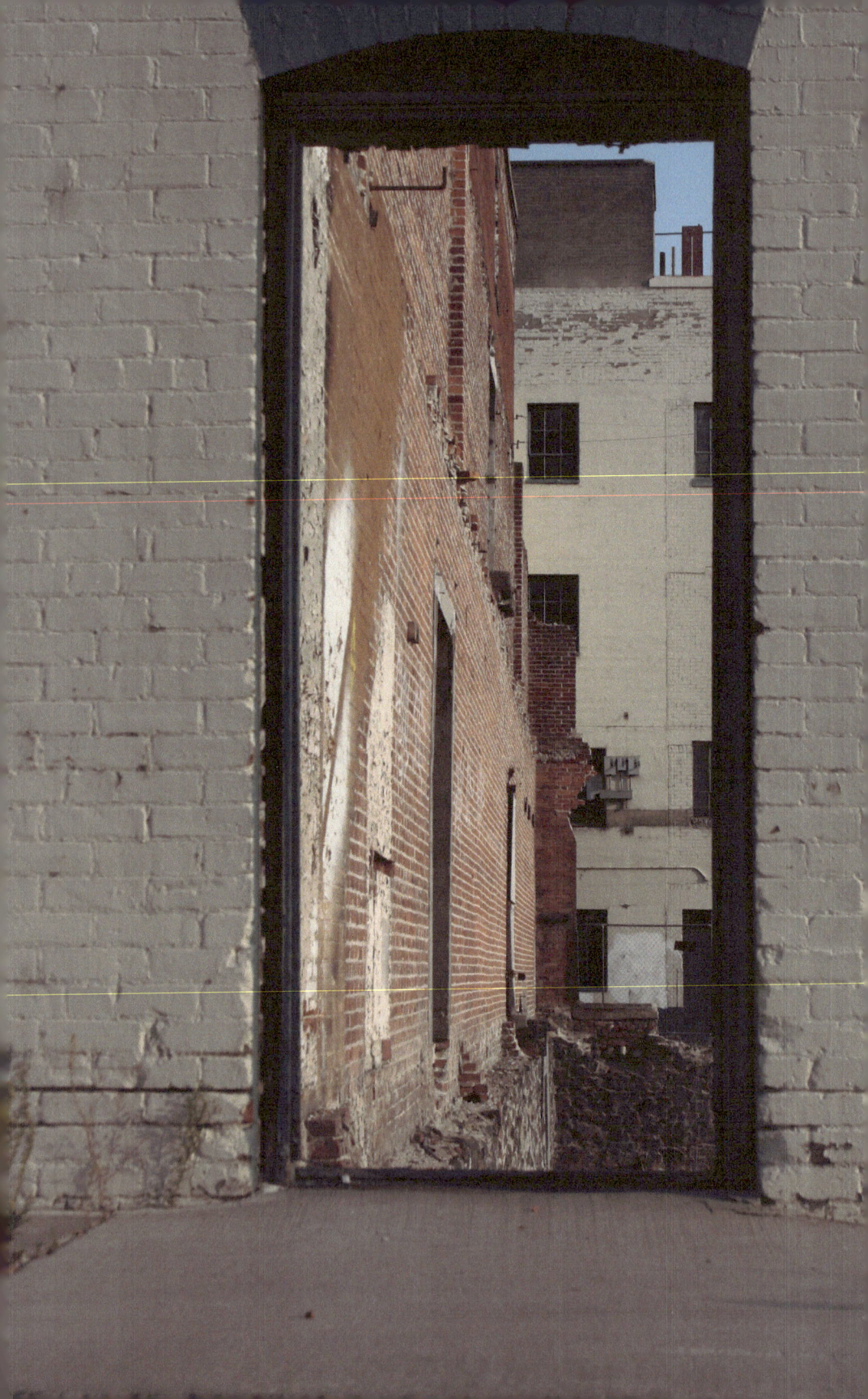

Big Mountain didn't wake Little Gibbon when the Pack Of Salivating Wolves came howling by, disappointed that Little Gibbon had shut the cabin door and that they couldn't break in.

Big Mountain didn't wake Little Gibbon when the Sudden Temperature Drop reduced the nighttime temperatures by thirty degrees.

Little Gibbon was safe and warm in the cabin.

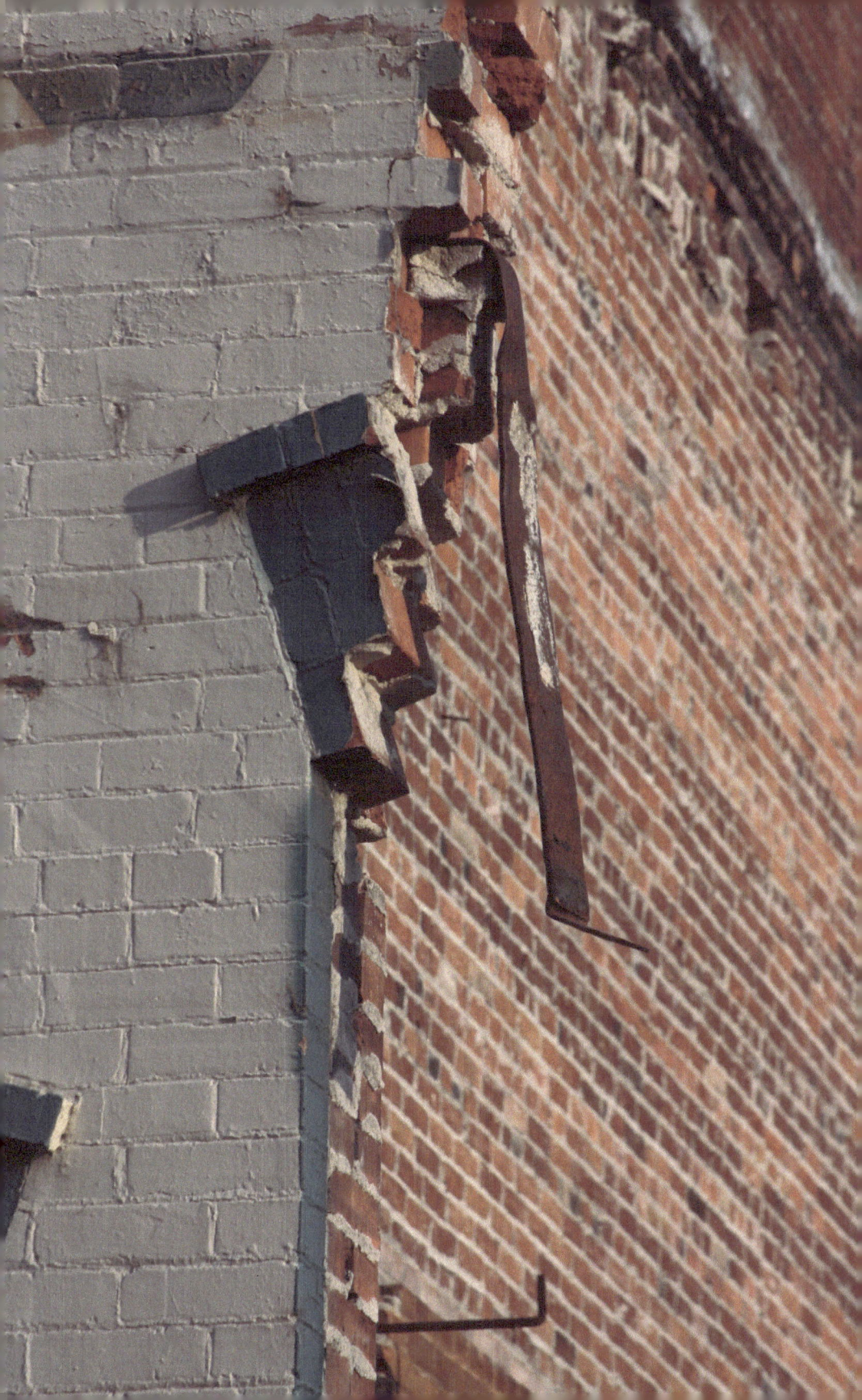

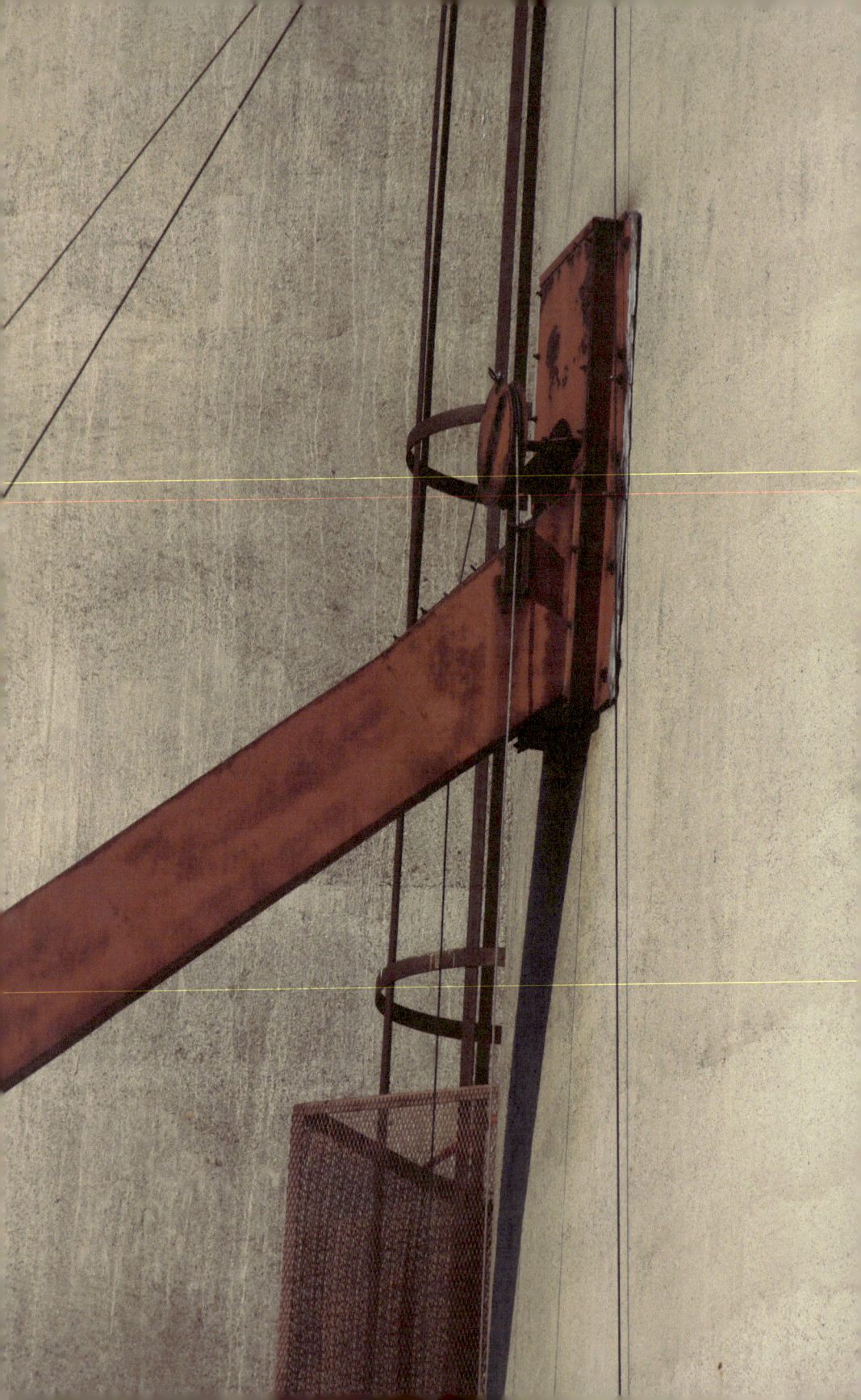

Little Gibbon had had enough adventures for one day, thought Big Mountain. There was always tomorrow.

~~

Reflection questions

If you could go anywhere to have an adventure, where would you like to go?

What can you do to learn about that location now, before you go?

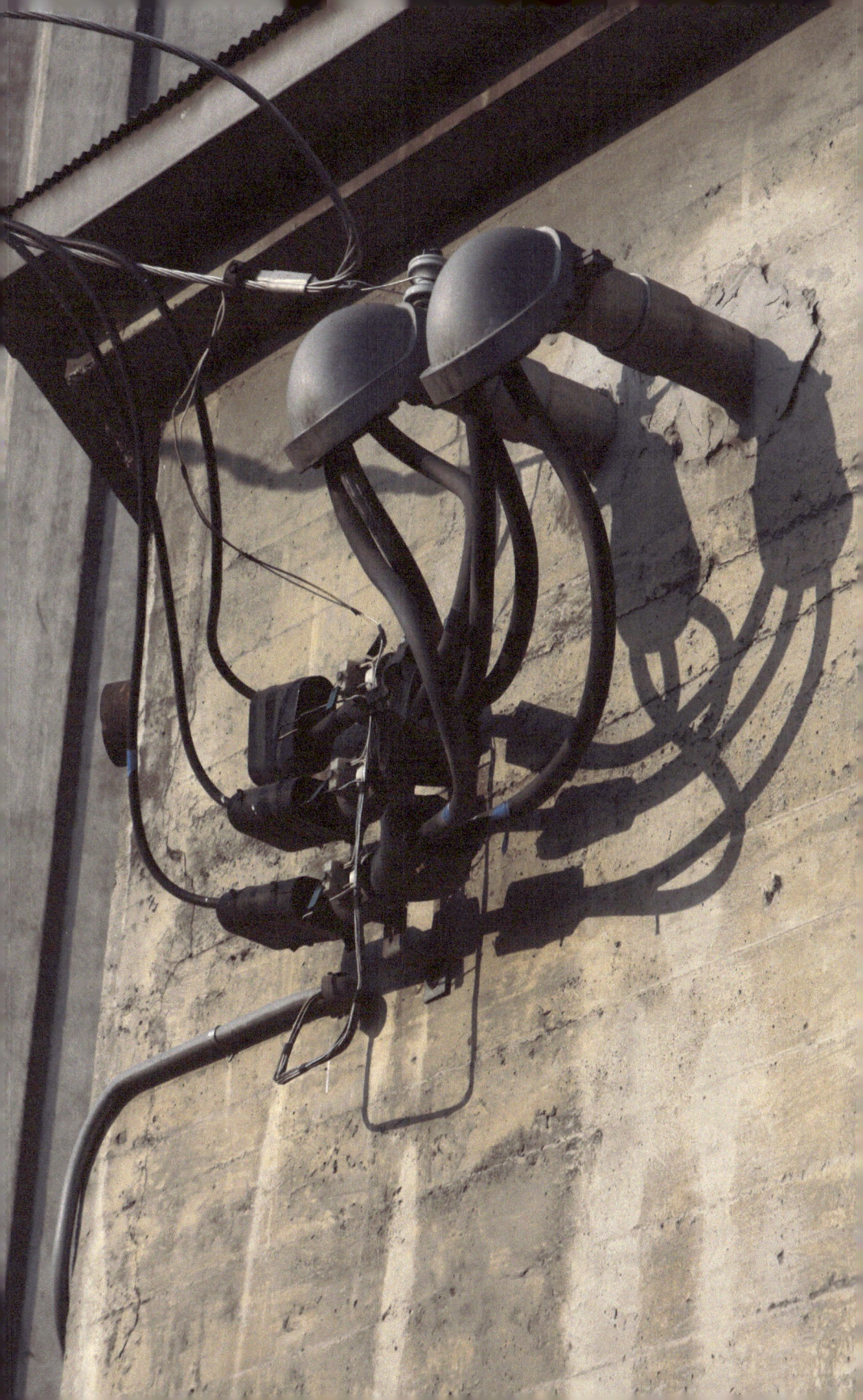

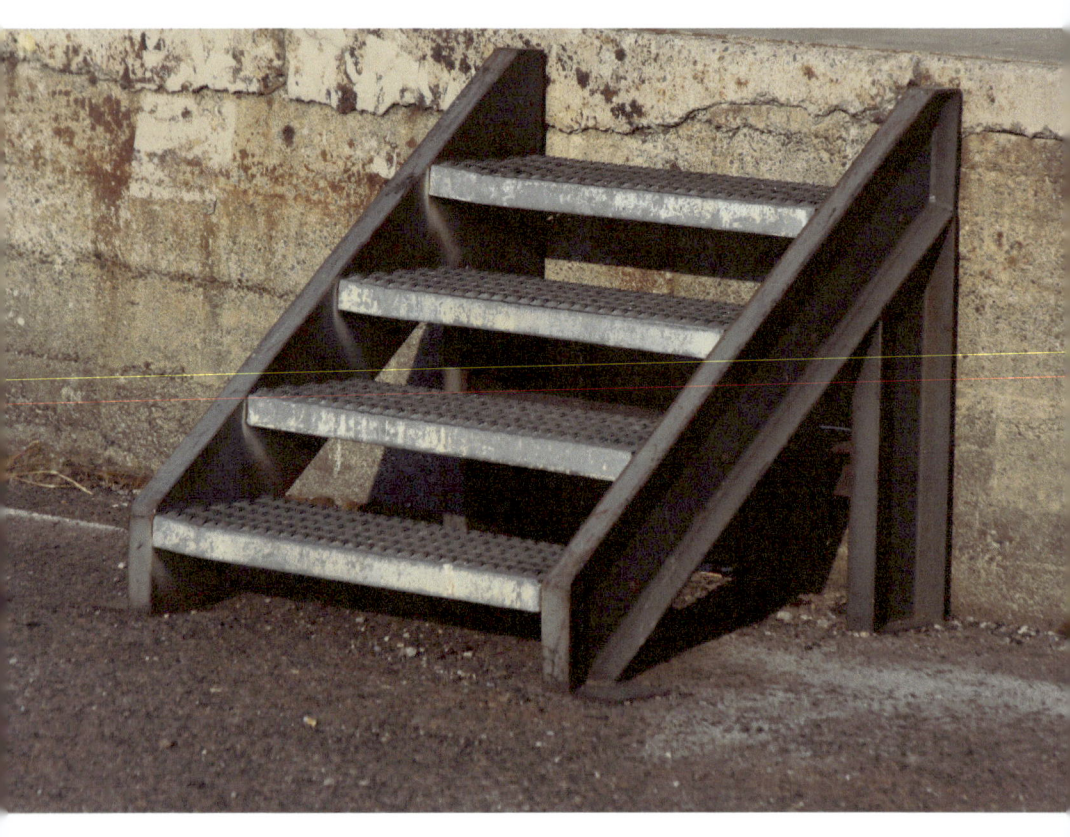

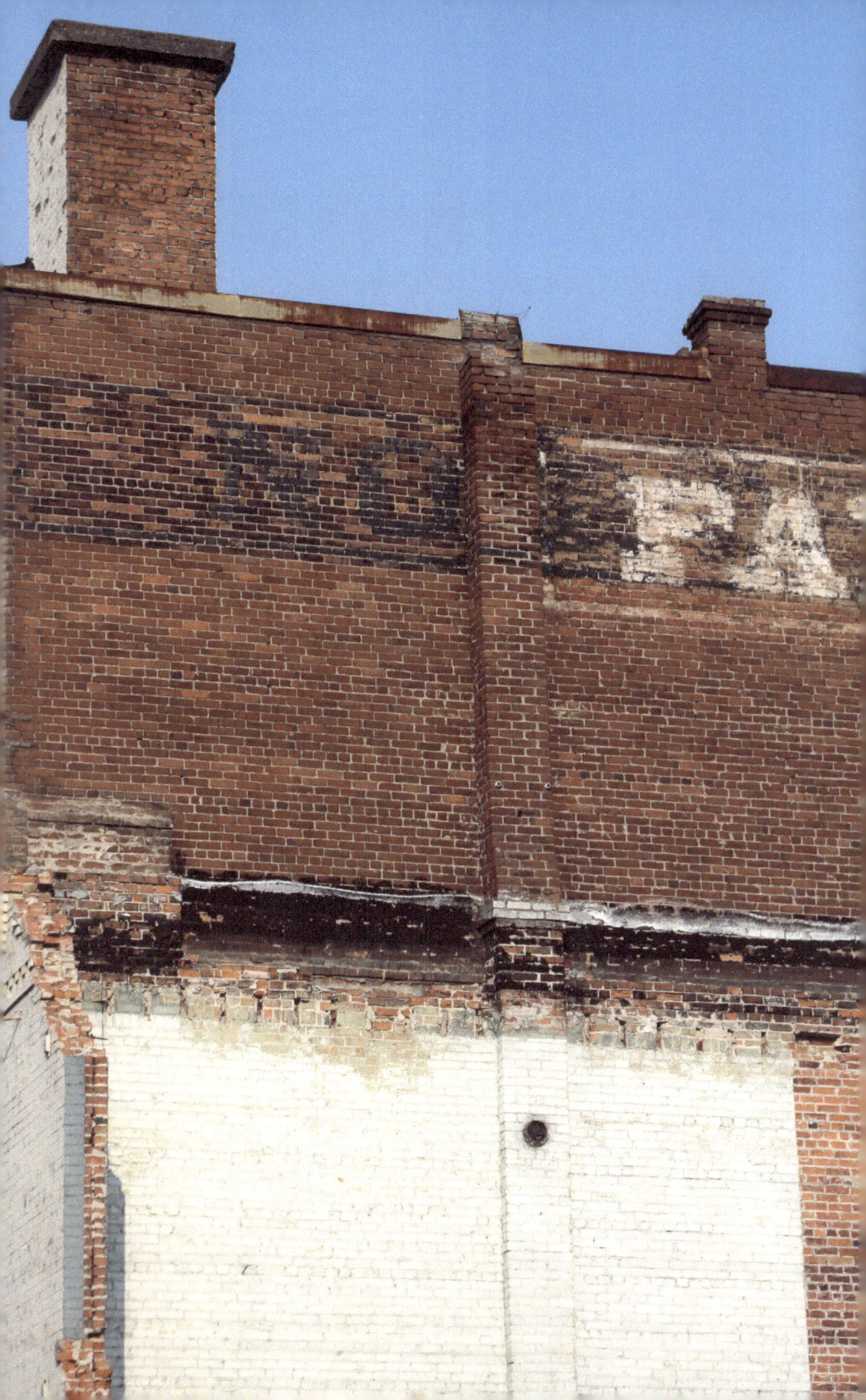

A Mark Dahle Portfolio

Monkey Brains In Big Desert

Little Gibbon's Big Adventures #4

This Mark Dahle Portfolio includes a photo of a colorful abstract painting, twenty-five outstanding photographs from Eastern Washington, and a story about a gibbon who liked adventures.

Little Gibbon had no water, no sunscreen, no compass and no sandals. He entered Big Desert smiling. Who needs those things when you want an adventure?

By now, you can probably guess what the answer is.

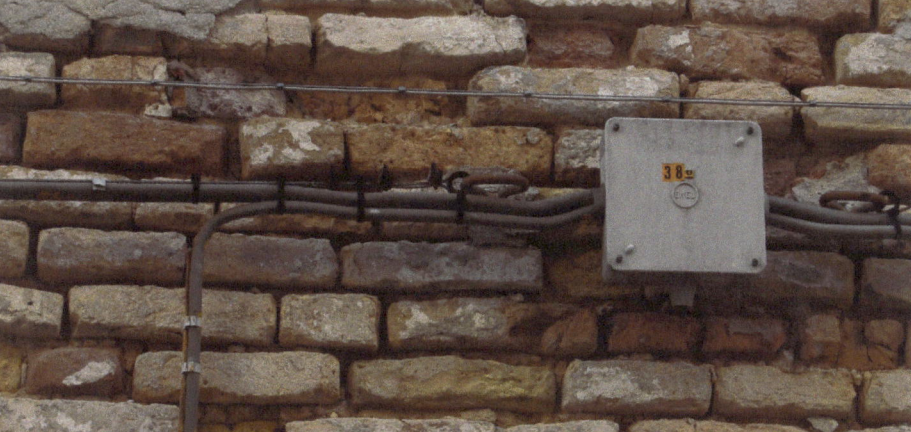

A Mark Portfolio

The Boy Who Loved Monopoly

This Mark Dahle Portfolio includes a colorful painting, twenty-seven beautiful photographs of Venice, and a story about a boy who loved to play Monopoly. One day the boy received $250,000 as an inheritance.

You probably haven't inherited any money this week.
But you've got lots of gifts
and lots of things that you're good at —
or could be, after you get more practice.
What will *you* do with all the gifts that *you* have?

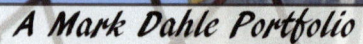

A Mark Dahle Portfolio

The Grasshopper And The Flea

Some Things Never Change

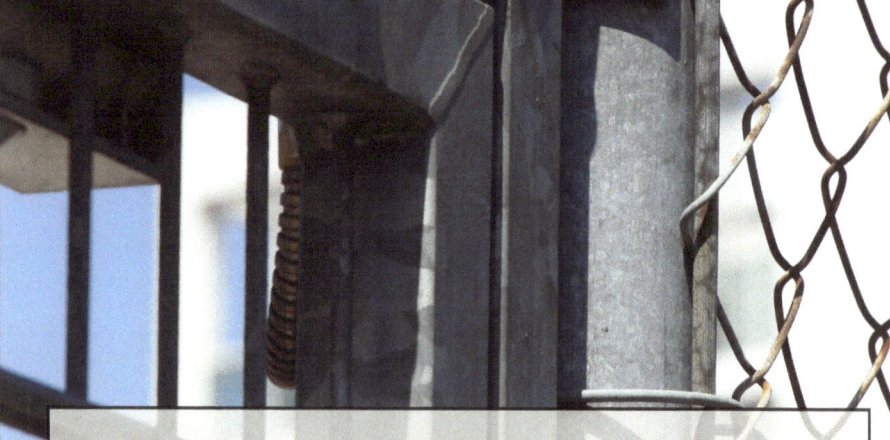

This Mark Dahle Portfolio includes a colorful painting, twenty-six beautiful photographs of fences in Basel, Switzerland, and a story about Aesop having remarkable difficulties writing a story.

Aesop liked the morals at the end of his stories to stay put. But he had just written about a grasshopper and a flea, and the moral was hopping around.

www.ingramcontent.com/pod-product-compliance
Lightning Source LLC
Chambersburg PA
CBHW040855180526
45159CB00001B/434